The Grass Is Always Greenest Under Our OWN Feet

Phoenix Duffy & Sara Anne Noah

This book is dedicated to healers, lightshifters, and spiritual seekers of higher truth consciousness and compassion and those who are interested in experiencing an uplifted and healed Planet Earth.

Balboa Press books may be ordered through booksellers or by contacting:

Balboa Press
A Division of Hay House
1663 Liberty Drive
Bloomington, IN 47403
www.balboapress.com
1 (877) 407-4847

Interior Image Credit: Carrie Bourgo

ISBN: 978-1-9822-4383-8 (sc)
ISBN: 978-1-9822-4384-5 (e)

Library of Congress Control Number: 2020903803

Print information available on the last page.

Balboa Press rev. date: 11/09/2020

BALBOA.PRESS
A DIVISION OF HAY HOUSE

Foreword

There is no greater obligation we have as humans than to mentor and guide the younger generations. That's what this book, *The Grass Is Always Greenest Under Our Own Feet*, is able to do. In addition, it also serves as a hopeful reminder to those who are aware of the New Earth Consciousness but are still struggling with some of the realities of the old paradigm.

The tenets presented in this work are not easily found in contemporary or traditional literature. Their basis comes from age-old wisdom, rediscovered by 19th-century New Thought philosophers, which includes some Eastern beliefs. The result is a rich collection of ancient and modern wisdom that can be united under the phrase, "Metaphysics."

Since meta means "beyond," the term "metaphysics" means that there are Universal Laws BEYOND the current physical understanding of physics, although science is slowly catching up. In this metaphysical story, the reader will find such principles in action, like the fact that our thoughts and feelings create our own reality. Such knowledge is the key to success in our world!

Science has proven that "Everything is energy," when broken up into its smallest observable particles. So it follows that we are all connected to everything, since we are all made of the same "stuff." How we treat ourselves, each other, and everything else has a greater impact on the world than we may realize. Reading this book will start to open one's mind to these deep ideas. And who is more open to new ideas than young people?

When I first started studying metaphysics at age 18, I wondered why we weren't exposed to such truths in school or in our places of worship. A bigger question is, why do most of us incarnate on Earth without being able to remember this information and our true purpose, until we're lucky enough to stumble across it during our lifetime? Or perhaps we do remember it, without understanding it, until we are school-age and the analytical, left-brain pursuits take over, or until puberty takes it away from our consciousness.

This book is an entertaining and useful "missing manual" that fills in what we have forgotten. It can serve as a guide to young people who may already be experiencing things such as auras and empathic tendencies, who may not understand what they perceive and why others around them don't perceive such things.

This is also a wonderful introduction to transformative New Age information, such as the healing properties of plants and the conductive capabilities of crystals. More than that, it can be the start of a lifetime of exploration and awareness of these metaphysical, Universal Laws.

Give this book to your favorite young adult reader, healer, or lightworker. Then guide a discussion on the principles contained herein. And be open to the younger ones sharing knowledge with YOU about these subjects! For this book may serve not only to educate them, but to reassure them that they are not alone!

Amy B. Garber
Director & Co-Founder, Enlightened Soul Center
Spiritual Counselor & Intuition Teacher, Metafizzy LLC
Senior Show Co-Director, Biannual Enlightened Soul Expo
Ann Arbor, Michigan
January 2019

Acknowledgments

We want to acknowledge our Source, God/Goddess, I/AM Presence, Jesus, Mother Earth, all the holy angels and saints, ascended masters, guides, ancestors and loved ones who supported us through the process of creation and manifestation of our book and movement.

A special shout out to Dr. Sue Morter and Rev. Michael Bernard Beckwith, who appear to us as Earth angels and teachers of New Earth reality.

A big thank you to our illustrator, Carrie Bourgo, for her dedication and amazing talents and gifts. Thank you for jumping into our creative endeavor and running with it. Thank you for sharing the divine feminine energy which brought our story to life and added immense value, love vibration and frequency.

Thank you to Amy Garber for her wonderful editing services and thoughtful foreword, helping us gain momentum in our movement.

Thank you to our publisher Balboa Press/ Hay House who gave us a platform to express this energy-shifting movement to life in a tangible way.

Thank you to every person who has donated & supported us spiritually and/or financially to get our book made. Special thanks to financial donors, Colleen and Curt Carstens, in honor of their children Ronan, Maeve and Shea. And special thanks to financial donor, Maria Alcini, who is honored to know and loves the authors of this book.

A standing ovation and thank you to the Aguilar-Olivera family who contributed a substantial financial donation in honor of their son. Thank you Guadalupe Astorga Olivera, Eliseo Aguilar and son, Eliseo Jr., who are all depicted in our artist's rendition of them in the Love Valley City renaming celebration scene.

We are so grateful to all of you who are reading this, and are ready to receive your blessings in broad daylight.

Phoenix Duffy

I would like to acknowledge my co-author, Sara Noah, without whom this book would not have come to life. Thank you for always moving us forward and helping me stay on track, and for your wonderful creative and positive viewpoint.

Thank you to all my friends, family, and healing clients who believed in me to get this project done, and offered many words of encouragement along the way.

I also want to acknowledge several dear writer friends who have transitioned on, and who helped me to remember who I am and to push through writer's block to my inspiration and motivation. Thank you to authors Mike N. Kelly, Mary Joyce Bowen Brady, and Brian Webster: Your legacy lives on.

Thank you to my twin flame, who showed me what it was like to be loved unconditionally, until I was whole enough to be able to love myself unconditionally.

Thank you especially to my parents, Mike and Betty Duffy, for your strength, love, and support.

Sara Anne Noah

Thank you to all my friends and family who have inspired me over the years to keep reaching the highest heights. My heart is filled with love for each and every one of you.

This book is dedicated to the loving memory of my dear friends Barbara-Jean Slopey, Michael Alexander Kelly, Lisa Shapiro, and Caiden Drake. And to my late father, Lynwood E. Noah, thank you for believing in me always.

To my dearest companion animal friends here and beyond the veil: Thank you for the greatest gifts of unconditional love, and the inspiration and belief in a future world that has widened the circle of compassion, so that all cages are empty and all animals are loved for the sentient beings that they are.

To my co-author, Anne (Phoenix) Duffy, thank you for sharing your lively spirit and huge heart with me and the world. This place is so much better with you in it.

To my dearest mother, Camilla Noah, thank you for being a role model of loving kindness, and for your tireless support of those around you. And to my sisters, Mary Lynn and Alicia, I am grateful beyond words for the support and love you have shown me my entire life.

A special word of thanks to people whose work and words continue to inspire me: River Phoenix, for carrying the messages of compassionate vegan living to millions of people (myself included), and Abraham-Hicks, for reminding me every day that all is well as I travel on this journey.

Introduction

There are children and young adults living on the planet at this time whose aura (personal energy field) is an indigo color, crystalline in appearance, and/or comprised of rainbow hues. These intuitive wise beings have come to this planet to use their light to shine on the darkness, to bring it into the light. So why not write a story to represent what is actually happening, to parallel real life? We hope this story inspires you to do your part in shifting your vibration within your own heart, changing your words, and by creating and holding light for the new collective paradigm to emerge. The New Earth.

"Bless this Earth for our bountiful garden!" Aunt Bonita exclaimed. "This garden heals."

"Aunt Bonita, my friend Lotus has a rose garden too!" Serendipity shouted.

"My child, this garden is a blessing in broad daylight. The herbs and the plants heal our family," said Aunt Bonita.

"Yep, the grass is always greenest under our own feet," Synchronicity said to her sibling, Serendipity. "We always have more than enough of whatever it is we need. Abundance is everywhere and everyone understands that here. We are so adored by our Source and so lucky to live here in the city of light, Starseed."

"That's right kids, you have many legs to stand on. Step up to the plate and receive your blessings. Life here is a cluster rainbow of opportunities, and we are all here for each other," said Aunt Bonita. "And pigs like Freedom get to fly."

"Aunt Bonita, may we add kikaujuana blossoms to our salad for dinner tonight?" asked Serendipity.

"Yes, certainly," said Aunt Bonita, "let me pick some for you."

"Kids, it's time to eat. Serendipity, will you get Freedom to the table now, please?" asked Mrs. Heavenridge.

"Sure thing, Mom. I'm so hungry, I could eat a whole forest!" Serendipity yelled, "Freedom, Freedom!! Get your sweetness together and come down here for dinner right now. You can always have your cake and frost it later too."

"Hey Dad, who are those people near the road?" asked Synchronicity.

"Hmm, I think I need to get my glasses on," said Mr. Heavenridge.

"Oh my, I know exactly who they are," said Aunt Bonita, concerned.

"Who?" Serendipity wondered.

"My oldest and dearest friends from Lost Valley, what are you doing here in Starseed?" asked Aunt Bonita.

"We narrowly escaped out of Lost Valley through the old mountain pass to reach you. Lost Valley has gone to hell in a handbasket and we need your help!" said the beautiful woman, named Hope Restores.

"What does that mean?" a perplexed Serendipity asked.

"The air and water are toxic and no one cares about loving each other anymore. We are dealing with demons every day. It's not all rainbows and unicorns out there, kids," said the man, Daniel Lyons.

"I don't understand. How can the water and air be dirty?" asked Synchronicity.

"Well, hon, not everyone cares for one another and the Earth like we do here in Starseed," said Mr. Heavenridge.

"Is my husband, Ray, okay?" asked Bonita.

"Husband!? You mean, we have an uncle?" exclaimed the kids. "Why haven't we met him?"

"Yes, I left Lost Valley to move to the nurturing and loving town of Starseed with your parents. Uncle Ray decided to continue his work there," said Bonita.

"We'll need an army of lightworkers for the whole town immediately. Ray's condition has worsened, and he is now using a wheelchair all the time. He needs the healing herbs of the kikaujuana plant right now, and is asking for you," Hope said.

"I'll make the journey," said Bonita.

"WE want to come too!" said Serendipity and Synchronicity.

"Oh no, we are not opening that... can of ... of frosting," said Mrs. Heavenridge.

"Honey, I understand you are concerned, but it's time. The kids are growing up, and they are ready for their mission. We knew this day was coming," Mr. Heavenridge reminded his wife. "They can't sit here in Utopia forever. Our kids are the wayshowers for the New Earth. We cannot stand in the way of God's divine plan."

"I know, I know... I remember now, but it could be dangerous there," said Mrs. Heavenridge. "I just hope their Divine Light can carry them."

"Of course Divinity will carry them. Let them go and do their life's work, what they were born to do!" Mr. Heavenridge replied, reassuringly. "This is what the world has been waiting for, and then we will reunite with our children once the Love is complete."

"Where exactly are we going?" asked Synchronicity.

"Lost Valley. You will get to see where your parents and I came from. Then you will understand the choices they made for you, to leave that place. It will be transformative," said Aunt Bonita.

"Can we tell the people who we are?" said Serendipity.

"No, we can't pull the hat out of the bag quite yet. We will stay with your uncle once we arrive. He is sick and needs our herbs," Aunt Bonita replied.

"What is sick?" asked Serendipity.

"It means the opposite of well," said Hope.

"When your uncle chose to stay back in Lost Valley, he wasn't able to be aligned with his true identity of wellness. It's so easy for us in Starseed, because we are surrounded by others who understand and believe in our divine birthright of radiant, vibrant health," said Bonita.

She continued, "You and Synchronicity have a divine mission with the people of Lost Valley. You will bring the elevated consciousness they need to witness. They will be able to shift to match their Infinite Source. You will be the balance that heals the camel's back."

"I feel weird. Is something bad going to happen to us?" asked Serendipity.

"That weird feeling is fear, honey. But don't fret, as nothing bad will happen. Not over my living, flourishing, healthy body," said Aunt Bonita. "The time has come for deep change and you, kids, are bringing your full light body presence that this town needs."

"I see smoke in the tunnel!" exclaimed Daniel, alarmed.

"My glasses are fogged up and I can't drive anymore," said Bonita.

"I know what to do! An Intergalactic Fire Drill!" exclaimed Synchronicity.

"What, huh?" said Hope.

"It's where you all get out of the car and switch seats. It's the rule of fun!" said Serendipity.

"This doesn't seem fun. There is smoke, look at the bats on the wall over there, and the dead canaries!" said Daniel. "You kids live in a bubble. This kind of thing happens all the time in Lost Valley."

"This is all part of the natural world. It's okay to see bats, we're safe and we don't know if the canaries are actually dead!" said Bonita.

"We should have taken the back roads through the mountains, the way Hope and I came to Starseed. It would be safer than this," said Daniel.

"Aunt Bonita, can we turn around?" said Serendipity.

"No, time is of the essence and I need you to come drive, please. This is all part of the journey and you are seeing the shadow part of life right now. We have a mission to complete and we will soon see what the divine plan is," said Aunt Bonita.

"I will bring the canaries to tend to them to see if we can revive them," Synchronicity said.

"Oh my God! That crazy explosion almost killed us and now we are all trapped here!" Daniel exclaimed.

"Oh, no worries, this is just a cluster rainbow of opportunities waiting for us," said an optimistic Bonita.

"Yes, you're right. Come hell or high water, we will find a way to get back," said Hope.

"You mean, 'come heaven and low tides,' we will get home again after we complete our mission," Synchronicity corrected.

"Yes, that's right!" said Bonita.

"Ewww," Freedom squealed.

"Oh no! The explosion must have broken Freedom's wing!" shouted Serendipity.

"That's the least of our worries. Look. There is a border guard who spotted us and he will want money and papers. Trust me kid, they don't like our kind here," said Daniel grimly.

"What do you mean?" asked a puzzled Synchronicity.

"Our light is too bright, and I am from a different time and place too," explained Daniel. "This could be bad."

"You can't punch me, that's illegal! This is wrong. I had nothing to do with the explosion of the tunnel," said Daniel. "You targeted me on purpose because I am different. But I am a respected professor at Lost Valley University, and I want to talk to my lawyer immediately!"

"Now Daniel, don't beat a dead horse! We've already heard that one before..." chuckled Chief Officer Hack.

"You mean 'don't feed a sleeping horse,' don't ya?" corrected Serendipity emphatically.

"Whatever, kid," said Chief Hack.

"Now there are many petals on a rose. This is all one big misunderstanding," said Bonita. "My husband, Ray Lightbody, is the Chair of the Environmental Ecology Department at Lost Valley University, but he is sick and we need to help him." She continued, "Please release all of us now! We have done nothing wrong."

"Ma'am, please turn the light down on your kids. They're shining too bright and we can't do our job. And what's with the green grass under y'all's feet?" Sergeant Heartless complained.

"Enough of this nonsense! They can go," said Chief Hack. "But that perpetrator, Mr. Daniel Lyons, has to stay and pay the price for damaging our tunnel."

"Thank you so much for coming here, Bonita. It's been so long and I have missed you dearly, my love," said Ray Lightbody, as he leaned in closer from his assistive chair.

"Of course I would come back for you, when it was the right time!" said Bonita. "I love you to wholeness, my love."

"And children, Serendipity, Synchronicity, it's so nice to meet you finally and to see humans in their fully activated light bodies!" Ray exclaimed.

"Yes, Ray, the time has come for us all to be in our full potential — and that includes you," said Bonita. "The children know no different. They have lived in New Earth energy their whole lives in Starseed. But they are now ready for their assignment and they're going to transform Lost Valley and everyone in it."

"This is amazing news! Since communication has been censored here and there is a travel ban, I have been unable to be in contact with you for so long. I am so grateful to Hope and Daniel for risking their lives to bring you all here," said Ray.

"What about Daniel? How can we get him out of jail?" Hope asked.

"Well, I have been working on a case about the frapping here that has been causing our water to become toxic. The drilling has also caused the mountain to be destabilized, and that is what caused the collapse of the tunnel, like a localized earth shake," said Ray.

"But the police are blaming it on Daniel, so they can keep frapping to exploit the rocks for their naturally occurring fuel," said Hope. "That energy vampire company, Violessence, is sucking the life out of the Earth here. It is all about greed. It's DISGUSTING!"

"What is greed?" asked Serendipity.

"It's an old belief system that's based on lack and fear, and we know from Starseed that is not true. If we work with the free-flowing energy of the Earth and the Universe, there is more than enough abundance of sun and wind and other forms of energy to provide power for all," explained Bonita.

"But isn't the frapping extraction poisoning Lost Valley's water? Don't they care?" asked Synchronicity.

"Yes, and some of us do care, and there is a declaration of truth gathering today at Lost Valley U. We need to go," said Ray.

"Bonita, my bones feel so much better since you brought the herbal remedies and medicated brownies. I can walk again and now I only need this cane! Thank you so much love!" said Ray.

"The kids harvested it, the kikaujuana crop," said Bonita. "And look, the canaries are alive and well, and Freedom's wing is almost completely healed."

"Yeah, I put the healing kikaujuana balm on Freedom and the birds, too, and they..." Synchronicity began to explain.

"Everyone! Stop this nonsense and get back to class. You can't fight city hall!" screamed Dean Clueless from the podium, interrupting Synchronicity.

"We want clean water now!" yelled Crystal, a young protestor who stood out from the rest of the group because of the radiant light beaming out from her heart and a patch of green grass under her feet.

"Beggars can't be choosers!" spouted Dean Clueless.

"Oh no! Yes you can elevate city hall and we will. Those in need deserve to succeed!" yelled Bonita at Dean Clueless.

"Hi I'm Serendipity and I am pleased to align with you today," said Serendipity, intensely gazing at Crystal.

"Well, speak of the angels. I am Crystal. I have been waiting for you guys, my tribe, to show up my whole life. Where have you been?" said a smiling Crystal. "I see you guys are standing on green grass just like me and our light together is magnetic."

"Hi, I'm Synchronicity, but what are you talking about, you've been waiting for your tribe?" asked Synchronicity.

"I've been waiting for others like me! The time is now. We must transform these people and this land to the New Paradigm. The young ones, like us, will lead the way," said Crystal.

"How will we know who is with us?" asked Serendipity.

"You will know who they are if they know the grass is always greenest under their own feet and you shall see the light shine forth the brightest from their hearts," explained Crystal.

"That's a really nice thought, Crystal, but we need to pick our battles and we have bigger fish to fry. I hate to play the devil's advocate, but let's get real," said Hope dismissively.

"Hey! I understand your skepticism, Hope, but let me play the angel's assistant here for a minute," said Bonita. "When you come from a place of joy and HOPE, instead of pushing away disharmony, it is easier to align with light. Then you can feed a fish and let it multiply."

"Wow, that IS my name... Hope," mused Hope.

"Yes, now you remember the truth of who you are. Let me bring you to a special meditation place that I used to go to years ago where you can feel empowered," replied Bonita serenely.

"Hope, we can choose our blessings and there are many cluster rainbows of opportunities. We can get Daniel released, the frapping stopped, and transform everyone to align with the New Earth, like we know in Starseed," said Serendipity.

"Ok, show me the way," said Hope.

"We have already experienced miracles with the canaries when the kids applied the healing balm, and the fact that Ray is without his assistive chair now, and Freedom's wing is healed," Bonita pointed out. "Won't you believe?"

"Yes, you are right, I should trust more," Hope admitted.

"This rose garden was created and tended to by my great grandmother, Rainbow Orion. She was a visionary and steward of the Earth. She knew the transformative healing vibrations of the rose flower, even back then," said Bonita. "We have all the tools to let God show us the way."

"Wow, my ancestors were creative and knew the truth of abundance, despite living in struggle!" exclaimed Serendipity.

"Yes," Bonita affirmed.

"I smell the fragrance and now I feel like I'm starting to understand. Oh my God! Look, the grass IS greenest under my feet now!" Hope said excitedly.

"Yes, and when like turns to love, you are able to receive your blessings in broad daylight, instead of a blessing in disguise, Hope," said Bonita.

"Wow, I feel like we have pierced the veil of illusion and we can now feed two birds with one scone," said Ray. "Look, Hope has found her alignment and I am well too. I don't even need this cane anymore!"

"Hey everyone, I have something even more exciting to show you! There is a secret crystal cavern nearby containing healing hot springs in it. It's where I received my activation to my expanded self," said Crystal.

"Oh, my gosh... what happened?! I'm devastated at the sight of this destruction. I feel sick," said Crystal. "My heart and spirit are broken. How can we ever possibly recover from this?"

"How did this happen?" asked Synchronicity.

"From the Violessence frapping. I have the proof!" yelled Ray.

"Wow, this crack in the cave is, I think, from an earth shake. It is probably connected to the tunnel collapse and the frapping too," Bonita suggested.

"So much for getting my hopes up. Now we will never get Daniel out of jail," said Hope sadly.

"No, no, don't drink the water, Freedom. It is toxic!" yelled a frightened Synchronicity.

"This is a fate worse than death. Even our sacred places are ruined," lamented Hope.

"Wait — all is NOT lost, I have an idea! We're from Starseed, and Synchronicity and I know what to do!" exclaimed Serendipity.

"See, look at the water change. Once you are enlightened, you are always enlightened, you just have to remember," said Bonita. "This will be the balance that heals the camel's back. Our light, vibrations, and love can shift the destructive effects created by those not in alignment with love."

"Serendipity, how would you know that the plants would transform the energy here?" asked Crystal. "Just sniffing the natural fragrance makes me feel hopeful again."

"In Starseed, we live in and have a relationship with nature, because we ARE nature. So each of us has the power to transform anything if we are aligned with Source," explained Serendipity. "The kikaujuana combined with the rose creates a quasi-surfactant that can help to clean the water."

"Watch this!" exclaimed Synchronicity. "I am also sending energy healing directly from my light body right now."

"Wow!" said Crystal.

"And, there once was a famous researcher, Dr. Emoto, who said water is the most receptive of all the elements to receive positive transformational intentions. Let us all focus our hearts and minds and use prayers to access the frequency of the rose to shift the toxicity of the water and repair the crystal cave," Bonita directed.

"Look, the water is already becoming clear and the cave is starting to sparkle!" exclaimed Hope.

"This is amazing! Who knew?" said Ray.

"Now, how do we get Daniel out of jail? I wonder how we can transform that?" Hope mused.

"Wait. You have mentioned him before. Who is Daniel and why is he in jail?" asked Crystal.

"He is my soulmate. Daniel works with Ray at LVU studying plant biology of the Andes. We snuck out of Lost Valley and took the treacherous mountain route to Starseed to get the Heavenridges and Bonita Lightbody to help us solve the problems here, but on the way back Daniel got arrested at the city border," stated Hope.

"Arrested for what?" Crystal asked.

"Well, I think he was chosen out of all of us because he is a man with darker skin and they wanted to blame someone for the tunnel explosion. Because of Lost Valley's historical belief in lack of resources, they won't stop corporations like Violessence from exploiting the Earth," said Hope.

"That's wrong! Well, where there's a will, Great Spirit shows us the way," said Crystal. "I think I know a way."

"How?" Serendipity asked her.

"I'm going to let the hat out of the bag here. My dad is the police chief of Lost Valley. I am certain that if I can get him here to this place, he will experience a healing alignment — and then he will do the right thing and let Daniel out of jail!" exclaimed Crystal.

"Wow, that is very SERENDIPITOUS that we met you!" Serendipity joked.

"Thank you so much! I love you to life," Hope said emphatically.

"But Crystal, how do we get your dad to come here?" asked Ray.

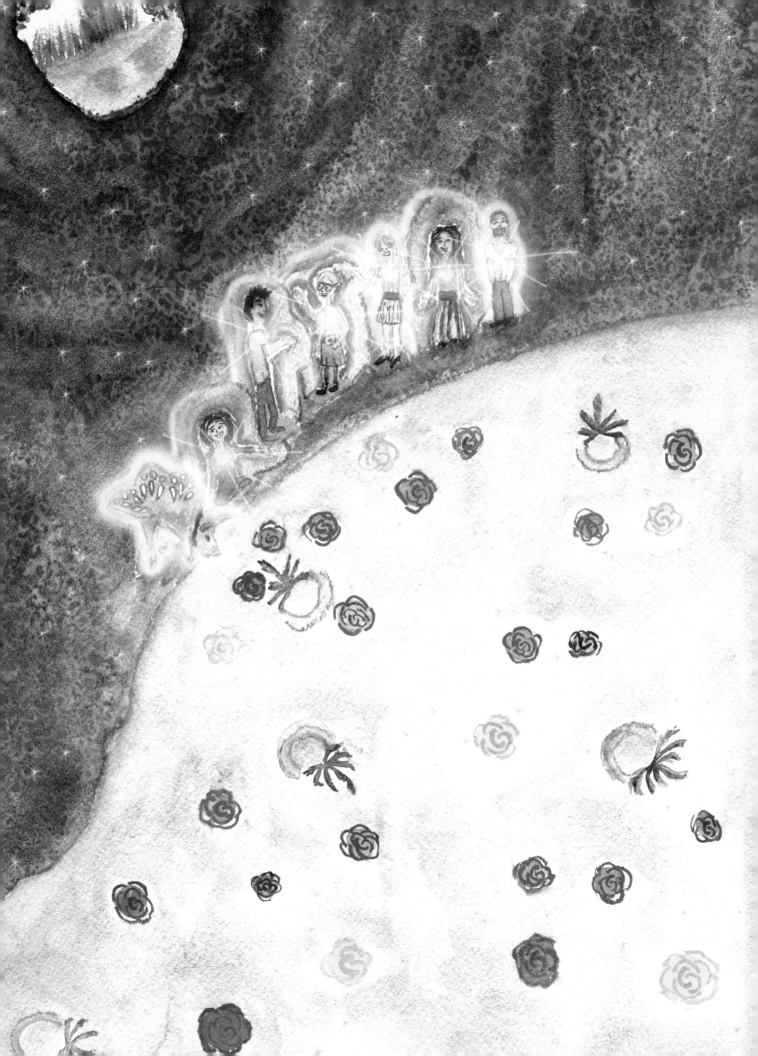

"Hi Dad! This bouquet is for you," said Crystal.

"Oh, what a surprise. For me? Wow, I can smell them from here. Thank you, honey. And a rose quartz crystal, it is beautiful! Just like when I named you, I saw a pink shiny crystal like this one in the woods and gave you the name Crystal... You look like you are glowing," said Chief Hack.

"Thanks, Dad. So much has changed for me. What are you doing?" asked Crystal. "You look so worn out."

"Oh, what I am doing doesn't matter. I am trying to make a case against this guy, Daniel Lyons, the perpetrator who collapsed our tunnel border," said Chief Hack.

"Oh?" said Crystal.

"Yeah, AND he brought these goody-two-shoes snots in from Starseed. They want to change how we do things around here and we don't like it," said Chief Hack with disgust.

"Dad! Those people are my friends! In fact, they are my kindred soul family. They are helping us be better people here!" shouted Crystal in disbelief.

"Young lady, I don't pay your college tuition for you to hang out with people like that. 'Soul Family'?" sputtered Chief Hack.

"Dad! STOP STOP STOP right there! That is Old Paradigm energy talking. We all need love and understanding right now, including you," Crystal said.

"Well, these are our values, honey," said Chief Hack.

"Dad, there is a better way. I need you to come with me somewhere now. It looks like you really could use a break. Do you trust me?" said Crystal authoritatively.

"Maybe," said Chief Hack.

"Thank you so much, Dad, for coming here," said Crystal. "I knew if you could be in the healing, transformative waters, feeling the beautiful energy of the crystal cavern and smelling these roses, you would understand and remember we are all love at our core."

"Well, I do feel different here," said Chief Hack. "It's amazing, like paradise."

"Yes, it's okay to let the light in and embrace the change Dad," smiled Crystal.

"Okay, honey, I'll try..." said Chief Hack in amazement. "It feels like the angels are here among us."

"You know, Dad, Daniel Lyons didn't blow up the tunnel. Professor Lightbody has the proof. The frapping company caused the damage," insisted Crystal.

"But the frapping company pays taxes to keep this town alive and pays MY salary," said Chief Hack.

"But Dad, it's the truth. That company destabilized the tunnel and they poisoned our drinking water too," Crystal replied.

"Well, you can't fight City Hall," her father said.

"Yes, Dad, you are right, you cannot fight city hall! But you CAN transform City Hall!" Crystal exclaimed.

"Well, if Ray Lightbody has the proof that Violessence caused the damage, then Daniel Lyons should be set free and I will get the frapping company to be held accountable," said Chief Hack.

"Thank you so much, Dad, for aligning with the truth! If you help us now, then you will be the straw that restores the camel's back. You are the change," said Crystal. "I'm so proud of you."

"Well, where there's a will, God shows us the way," said her father.

"Greetings citizens! Today is a great day," said Peace Officer Chief Hack. "We would like to thank those who helped us vote for our new name, LOVE VALLEY, including Violessence, who paid for the renaming process and the re-beautifying of this park. But we especially would like to thank our visitors, Serendipity, Synchronicity, Bonita and Freedom, who risked their lives to show us how to make healthier choices for our future generations. I am pleased that my daughter, Crystal, welcomed them with open arms. We feel terrible for the persecution of Daniel Lyons and what he had to endure. Today we are giving Daniel Lyons a key to the city, and a grant for $100,000 to continue his study of the wisdom of plant medicine. Because he had to sacrifice his freedom for a short while as we were challenging and in the process of changing our old beliefs, outdated policies, and biased laws, we fully apologize from the depth of our hearts. In addition, we also have deep gratitude for the risk that Hope Restores and Daniel took in order to get outside help for Lost Valley to receive the transformational healing upgrade to Love Valley."

"And furthermore, everybody here now has made the choice to align with compassion, loving, expansive, and forgiving energy that was always present here but was not being acted upon previously. It took visitors from our beloved and now sister city of Starseed to show us this. Let's give a round of applause for Synchronicity Heavenridge, who is representing the group from Starseed," said Peace Officer Chief Hack.

"Hello, Love Valley!" Synchronicity greeted the crowd. "I came from Starseed with my family and I was so unaware of the struggles that existed here when I ventured on this journey. I feel so blessed to be a part of what has transformed here."

She continued, "I am grateful to my parents, the Heavenridges, and to my aunt and uncle, the Lightbodys, who allowed me and my sibling, Serendipity, to live out our divine mission as rainbow children and wayshowers for the New Paradigm transformation here. And thank you Chief Hack for your willingness to trust us as you opened your heart to the possibilities of change. I wish you all joy and true freedom as your city embraces its natural abundance and success and new name!"

Chief Hack exclaimed, "Children of all ages should be seen, heard, respected, revered, and adored. They hold the light for our bright future. Now let us dance and celebrate as we finally recognize that THE GRASS IS ALWAYS GREENEST UNDER OUR OWN FEET! I love you all and I love this town."

"Hey, what about Lackland and the people there? Will the grass ever be greenest under THEIR feet?" asked Serendipity.

"Oh, that? I put kikaujuana blossoms, roses, and crystals from the hot springs cave in their bus when they weren't looking. We should always keep creating bridges," laughed Crystal. "It's only a matter of time before THEY start feeding two birds with one scone."

THE END

To hear the song "School of Love" being played at the celebration please tune in to YouTube channel bunnyhugger333

Author Bio – Phoenix Duffy

Phoenix Duffy, born and raised in Michigan, holds a bachelor's degree in biology from Wayne State University in Detroit, Michigan and an associate's degree in journalism and a certificate in digital video from Washtenaw Community College in Ann Arbor, Michigan.

Additionally, she is trained as an intuitive energy healer/coach for over 20 years. She is excited to share some of the healing concepts in this storybook. Phoenix loves to meditate and visit the beach often.

She lives with her Siamese flame point cat, Cupcake, in the San Francisco Bay Area, a dream she had since she was 13 years old. Phoenix continues to work with others, helping to support and hold space for them on their healing journey and she is enjoying spending time writing more books and movie scripts.

Author Bio - Sara Anne Noah

Sara Anne Noah was born and raised in southeastern Michigan and loved growing up in the country. She received her master's degree in interdisciplinary studies from Naropa University in Boulder, Colorado and her bachelor's in arts management from Eastern Michigan University in Ypsilanti, Michigan. Sara worked for almost two decades in higher education, primarily in student services & advocacy.

Sara is excited about yoga, meditation, kirtan, songwriting, vegan foods, animal rights, and spending time in nature. She is looking forward to completing many more creative projects in the future.

Illustrator Bio – Carrie Bourgo

Carrie Bourgo is a watercolor artist. Her passion is helping modern day mystics to gain insight and clarity into their innate divine connection through symbolic watercolor painting that embodies the deep love and emotion experienced during the transformational journey of the soul.

She currently resides in Southern Wisconsin with her husband, their three children, and dog.

www.etsy.com/shop/CarrieLBourgo

Please like us on Facebook: The Grass Is Always Greenest Under Our Own Feet Book Fans and Instagram: @thegrassisalwaysgreenest

Printed in the United States
By Bookmasters